The Music Beneath Her Skin

A Collection of Photographic Poetry

words and edits by Jacob Russell Dring

Copyright © 2019 by Jacob Russell Dring

original photographs courtesy of *santababydelasflores*
additional edits by Jacob Russell Dring

All rights reserved. This includes the right to reproduce this book or portions thereof in any form whatsoever, except in the case of excerpts used in cited reviews. Therefore unauthorized or uncited reproduction of any part of this work is illegal and punishable by law.

Printed in the United States of America.

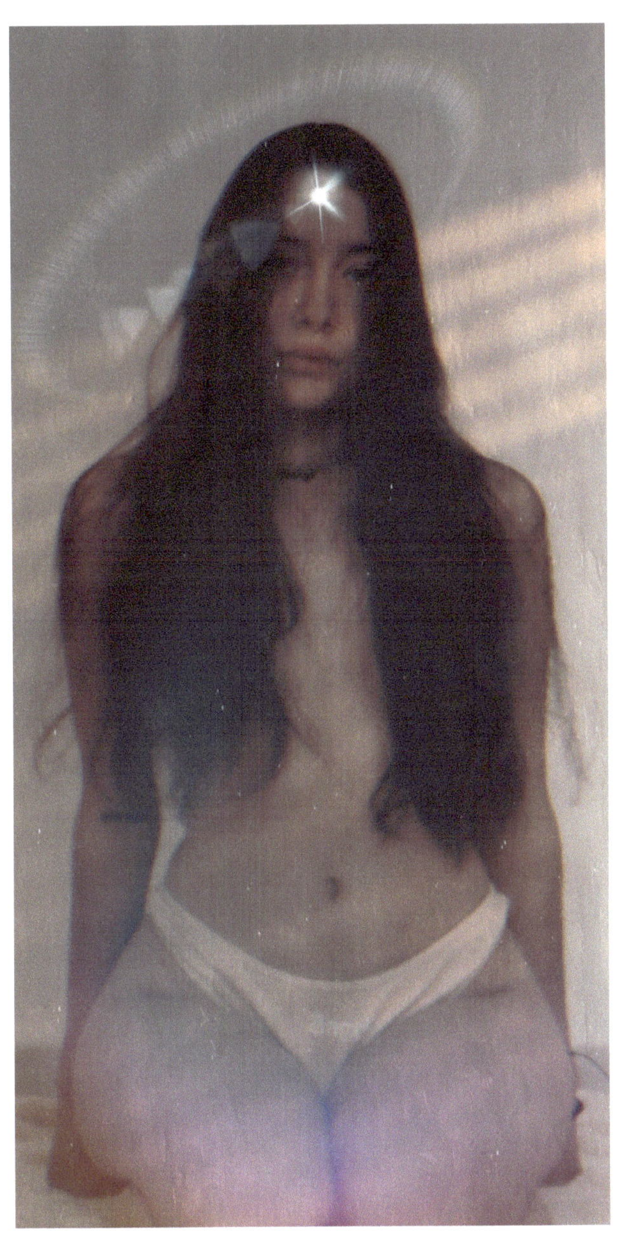

Flower angel, halo brain
thoughts so divine, to taste your lips
would be to caress the gods

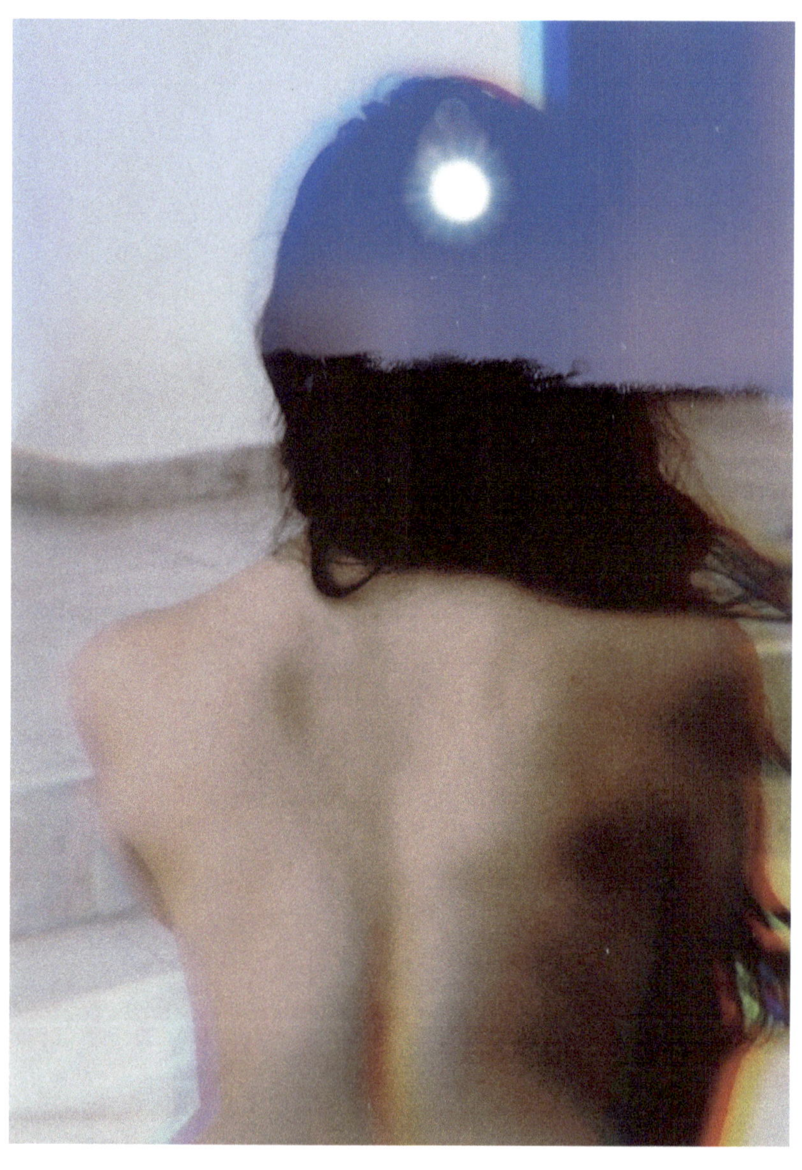

They say "follow your heart"
but I just want to chase her moon.
Besides, in a midnight sky like hers,
how could I not be captivated?

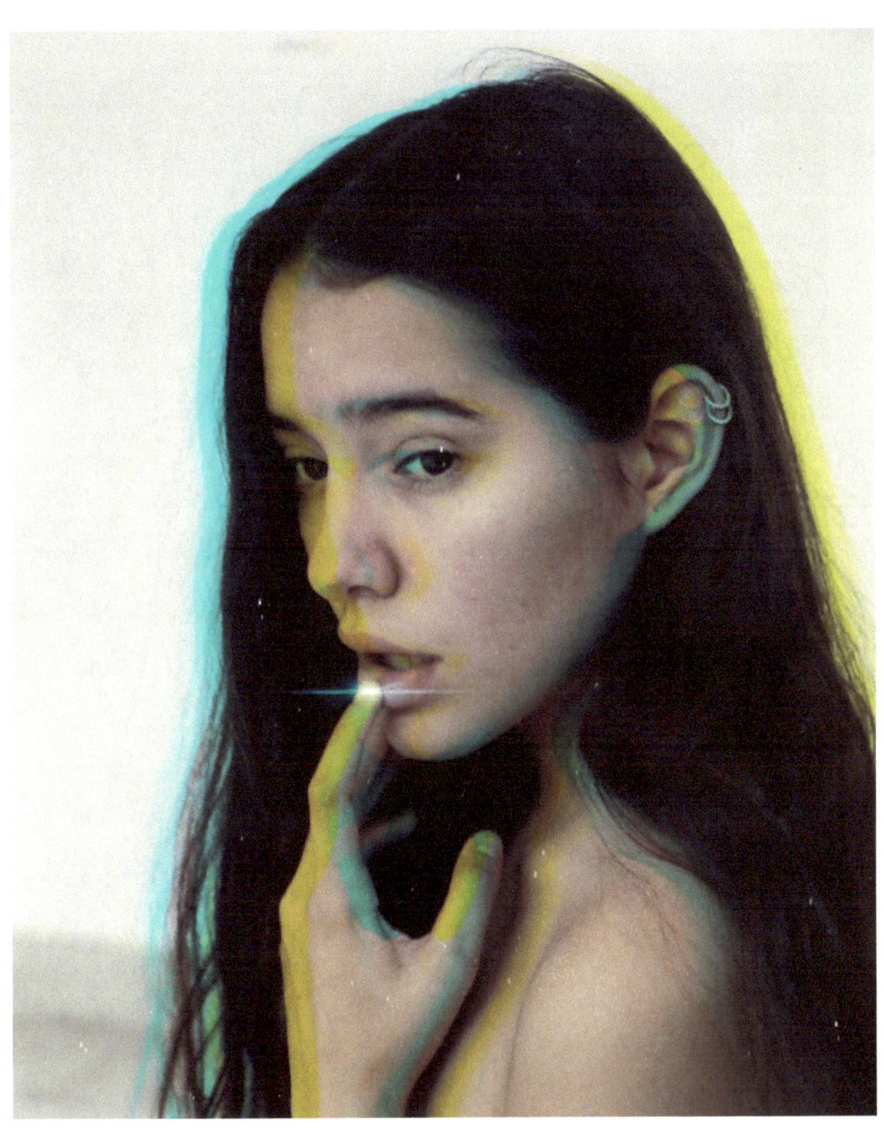

Interstellar flavor, a morsel of hope
I look at you and immediately know
we aren't alone in the universe

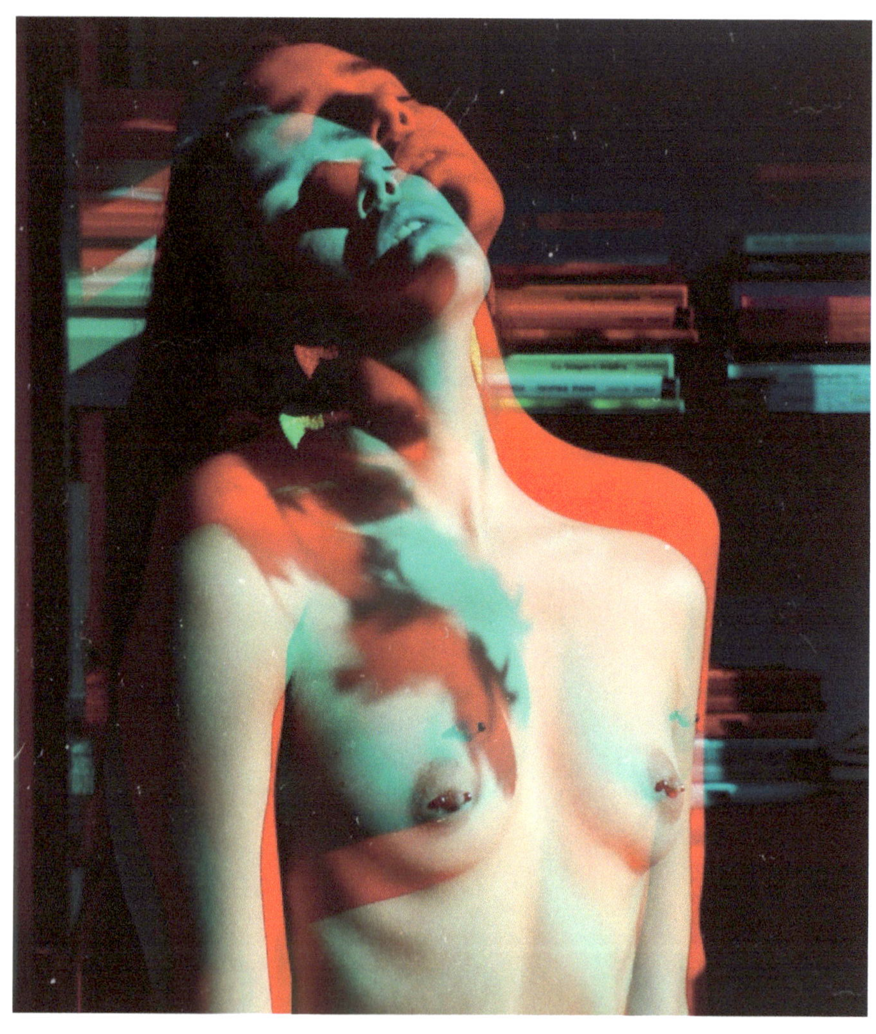

Abandon this dimension, embrace ascension
the serenity in your veins comes from a higher plane
can't you hear it sing your name?
answer with acceptance:
such a beautiful fucking exodus

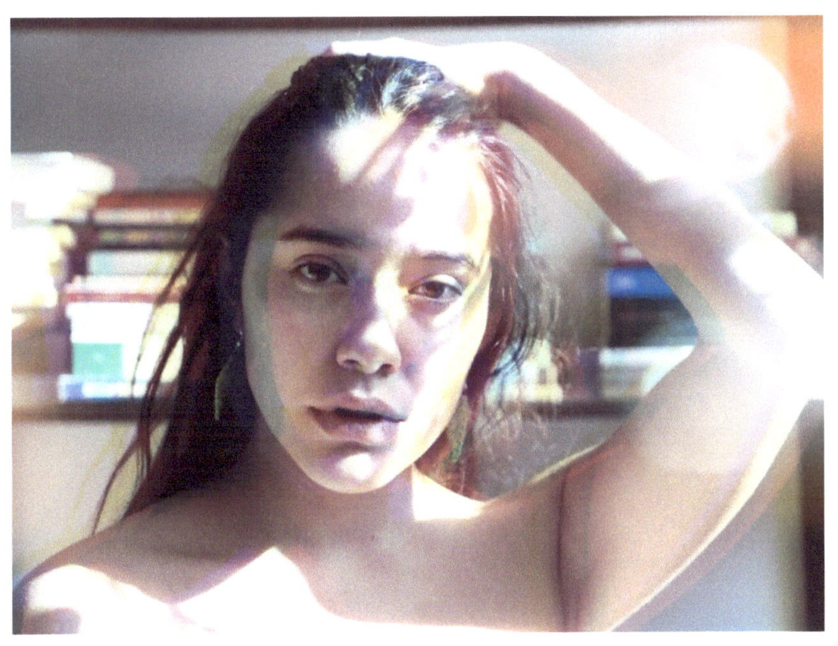

Daydream eyes
I am caught in your net
softly immured
but not prohibited
from drifting off
through honey seas
in your sight

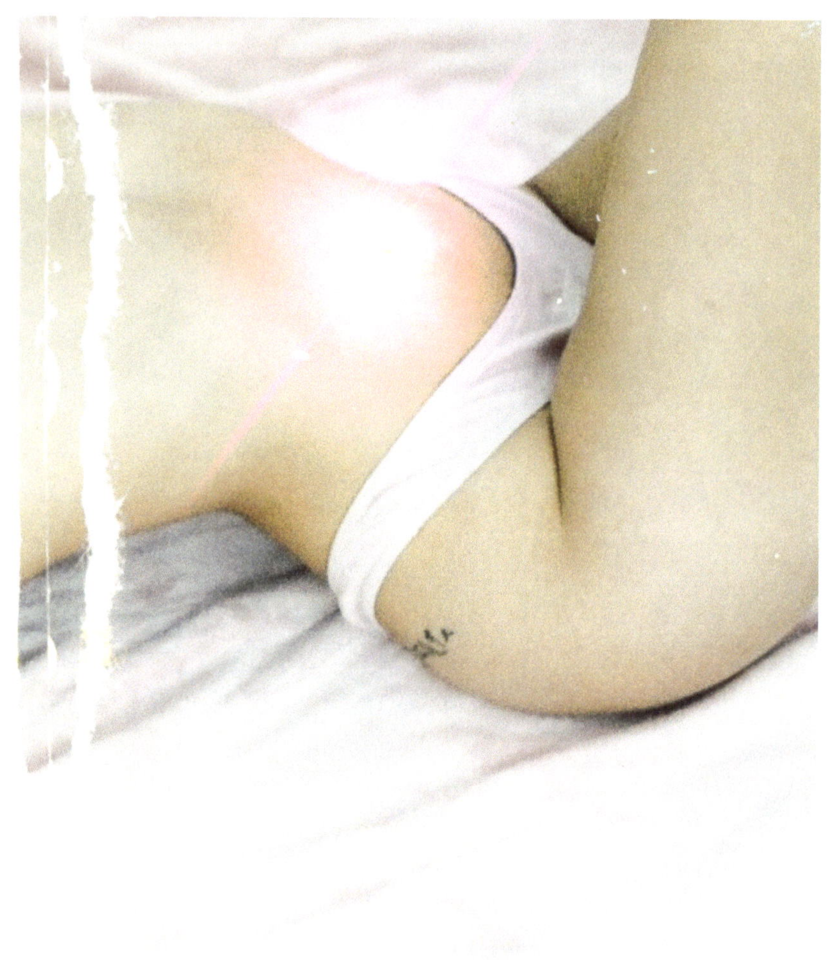

From the womb of paradise, you were taken
but this realm is forever grateful to be graced
by the silken, feminine beauty of your form
and the light pouring from within

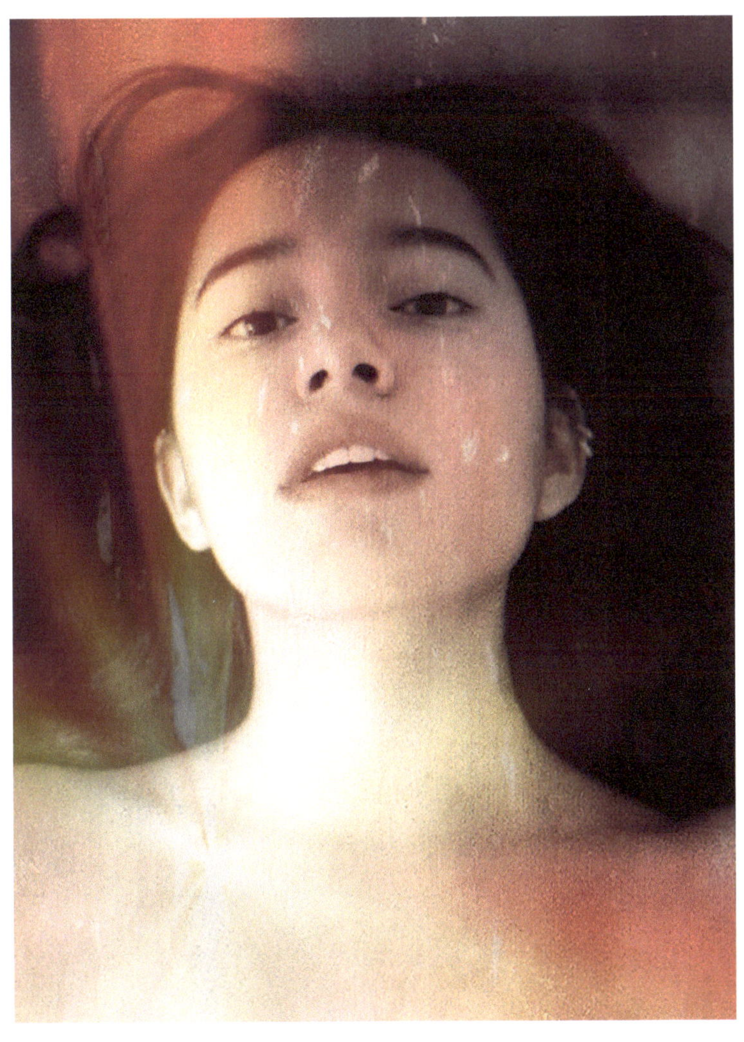

Let it wash over you, the warmth of freedom.
Let it devour you, the heat of rapture.
Embrace weightlessness as you float above the flames.

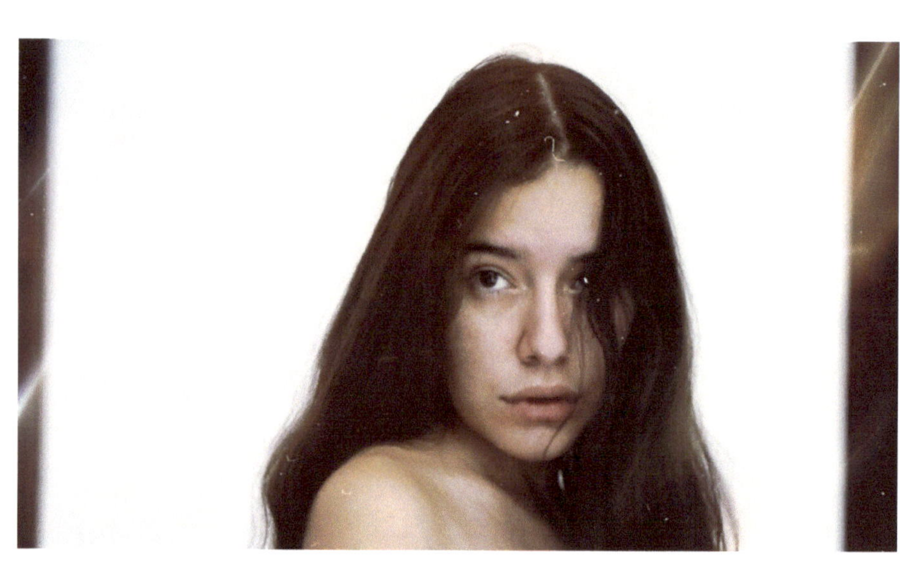

Like a gentle moon
your reflection
is what saves me
from certain doom.

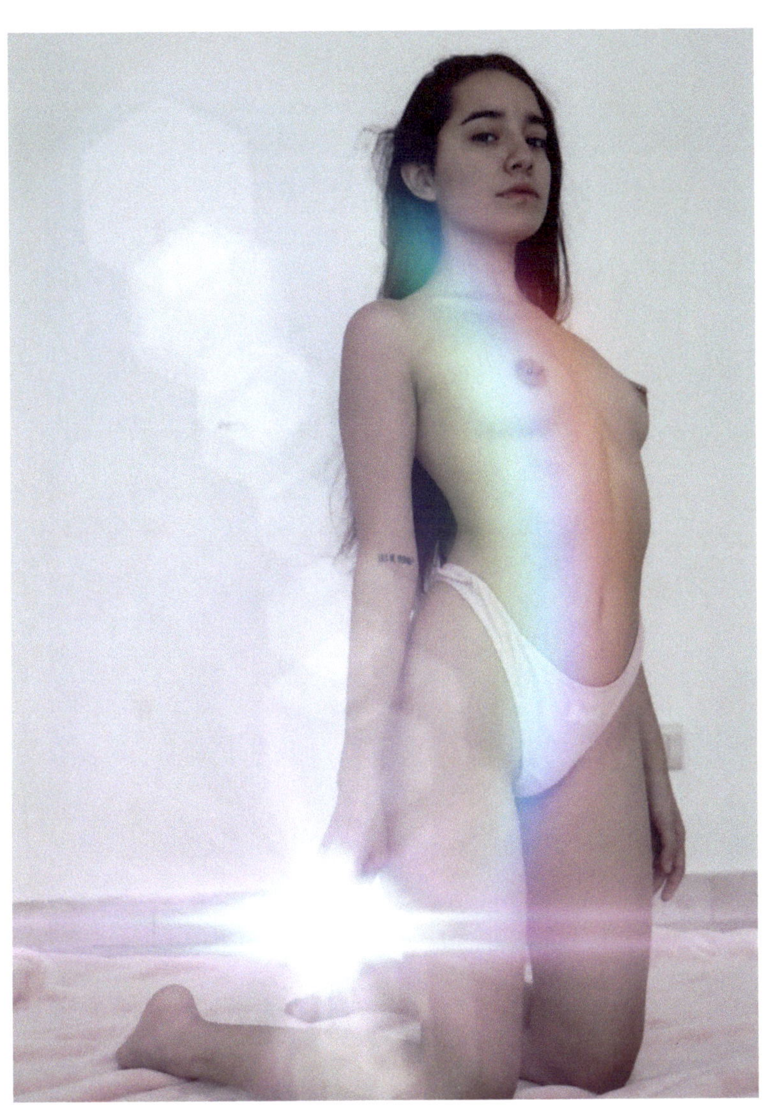

Oracle, please show me the way.
Bless my flesh with your beacon touch.
I want to bathe in the illumination
that you so often don't realize is yours.
It is a part of you; Inseparable.

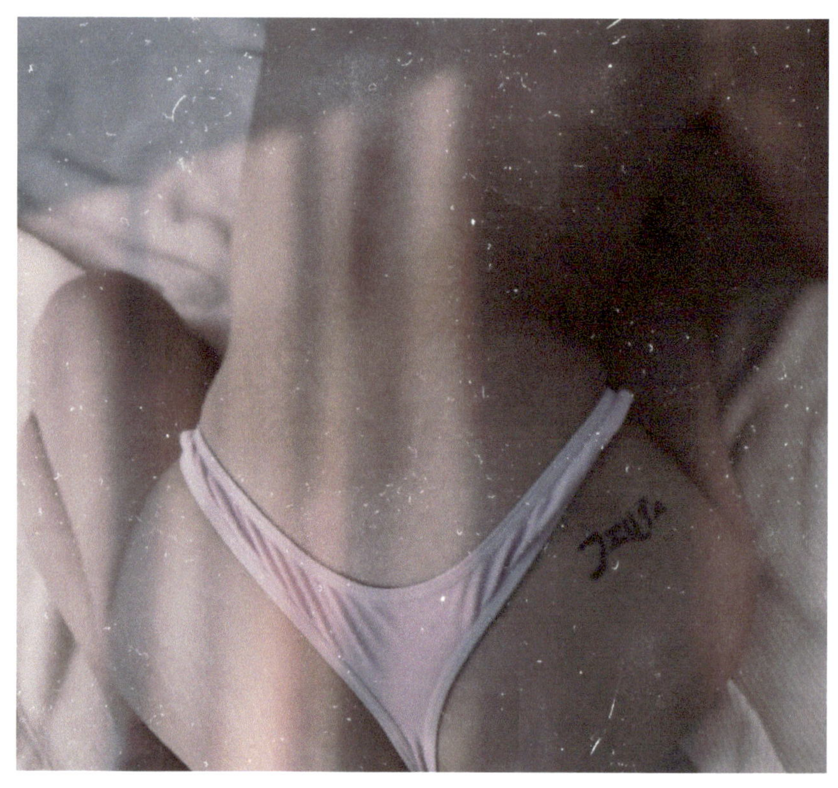

Sunset mountains
paint her skin
in hues of mist
and wet breath
like watercolor

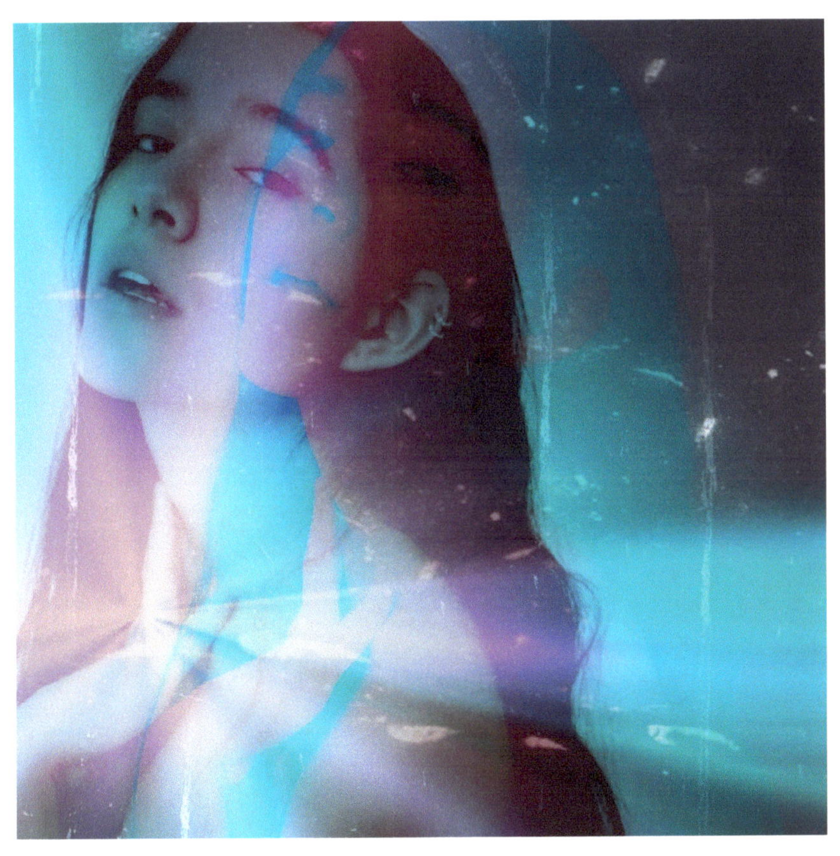

To taste the music
brewing in your throat
rising from your lungs
conducted by your heart
would be to savor a symphony
extracted from another galaxy
plucked from dying stars
and singing, begging
for a fresh eternity

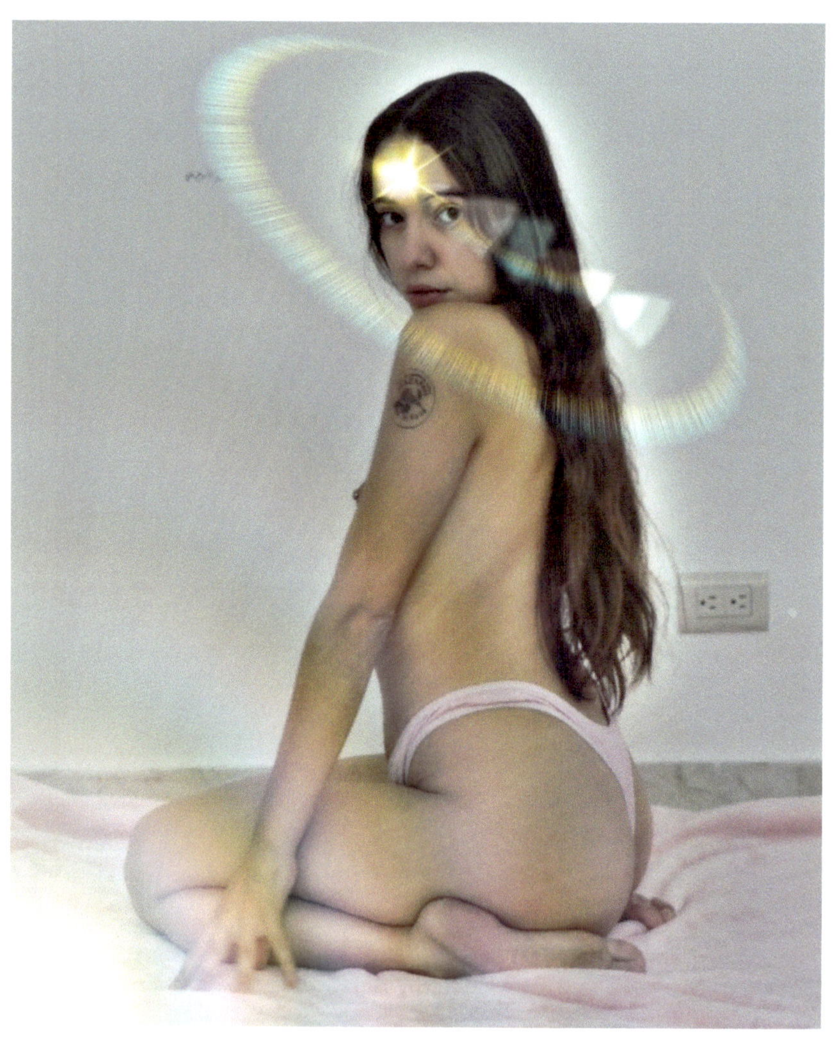

I see beyond the flesh in your bones
past the skin on your blemishes
I see the light in your darkness
the fortitude in your frailty
the angels in your demons

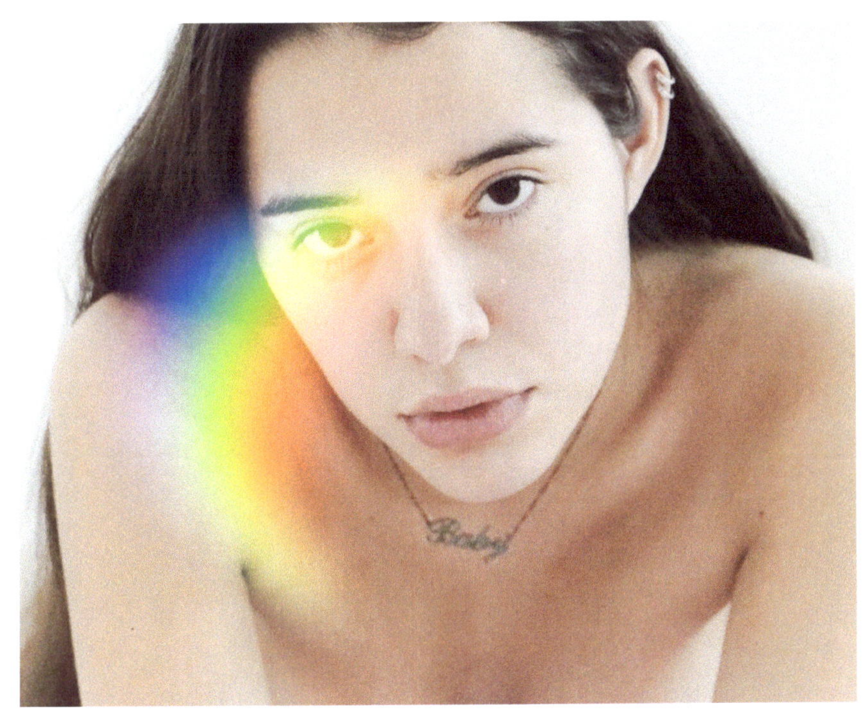

Cast beneath your glow,
I bathe weightlessly
under your anvil eyes.
How can I repay you?
I'd sell my soul just to see
where your colors
come from.

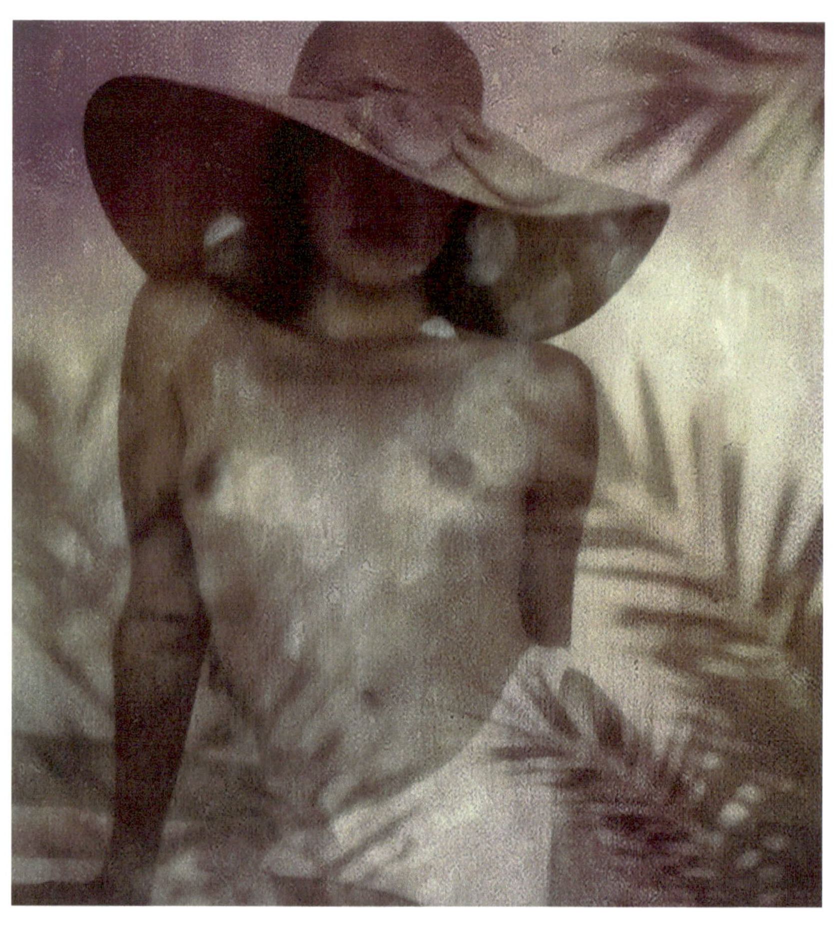

The waves crash gently ashore,
reminding me of the melody
akin to how you move.
Your body is a note
that no instrument can perform.
Even when sitting still,
you're a halcyon tempest:
the perfect paradise.

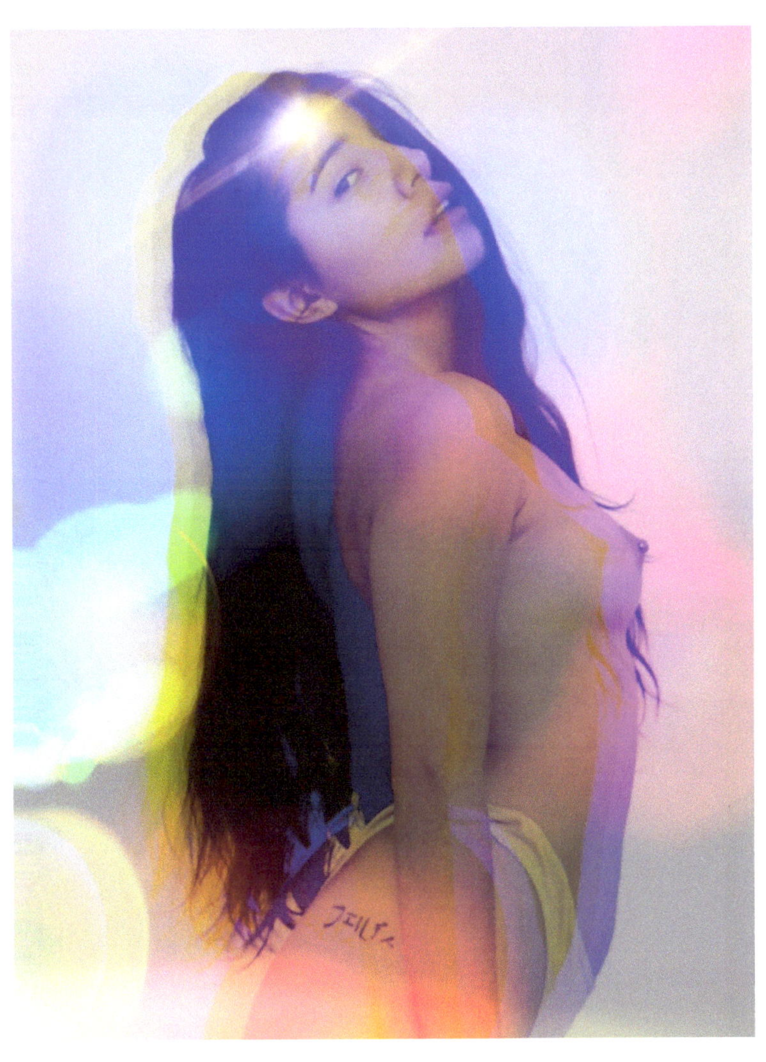

When our eyes meet
I elevate to a higher plane
yet you levitate above me
unfettered by physical restraints
like light passing through a window pane

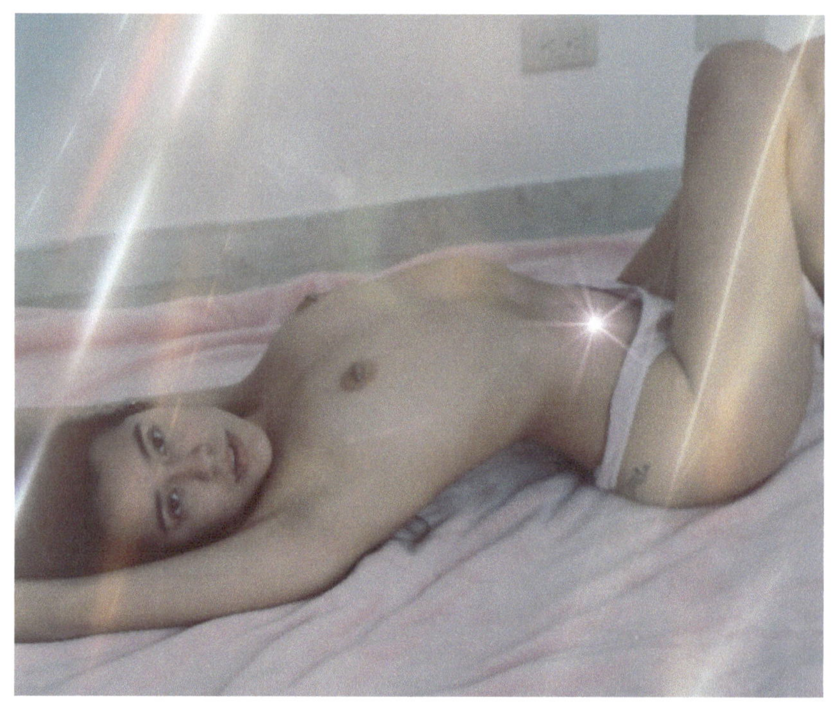

Breathe in, breathe out...
Watch her beauty like art
fluctuate but never mitigate.
I observe from outside myself,
doused in an intoxicating softness.

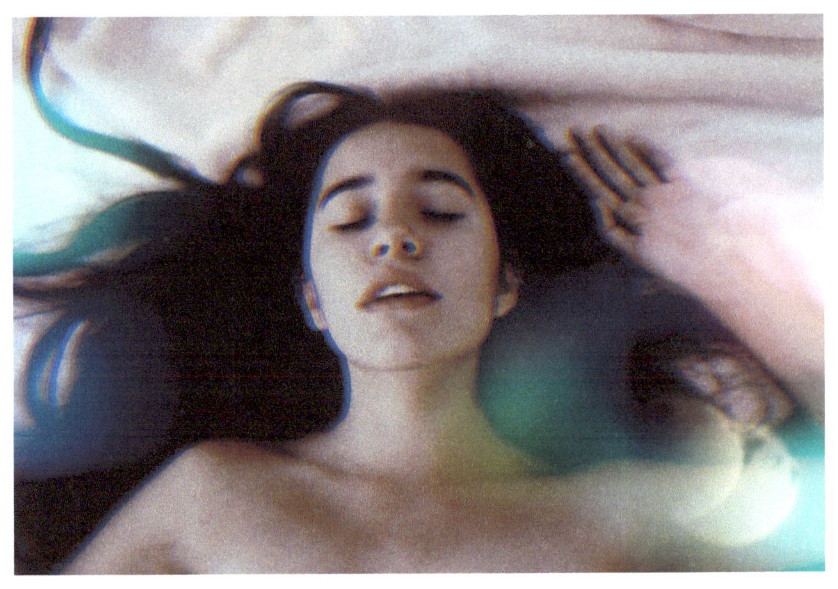

Mauve moonlight
teeming on your lips;
you don't experience rapture,
rapture experiences you.

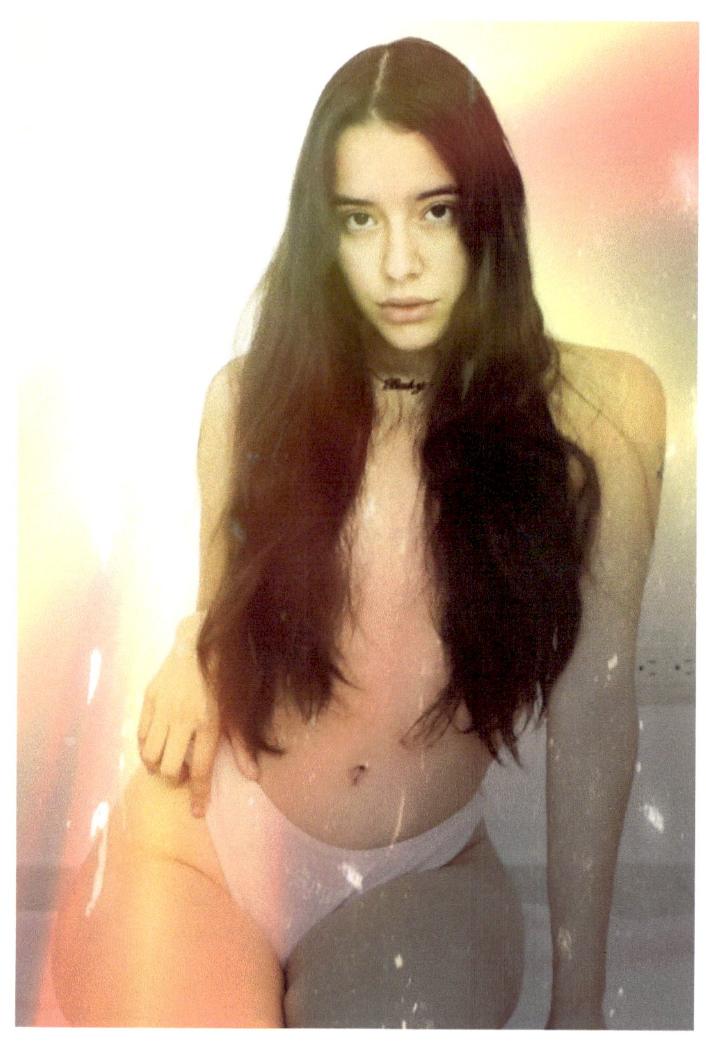

The supple darkness in your unabashed eyes
and the velveteen curvature
of your unapologetic vessel
produces an energy dancing through the air
like embers on the wind, like petals in a storm
and not unlike the hot center of any raging flame
the sight of you alone makes me feel...unstoppable

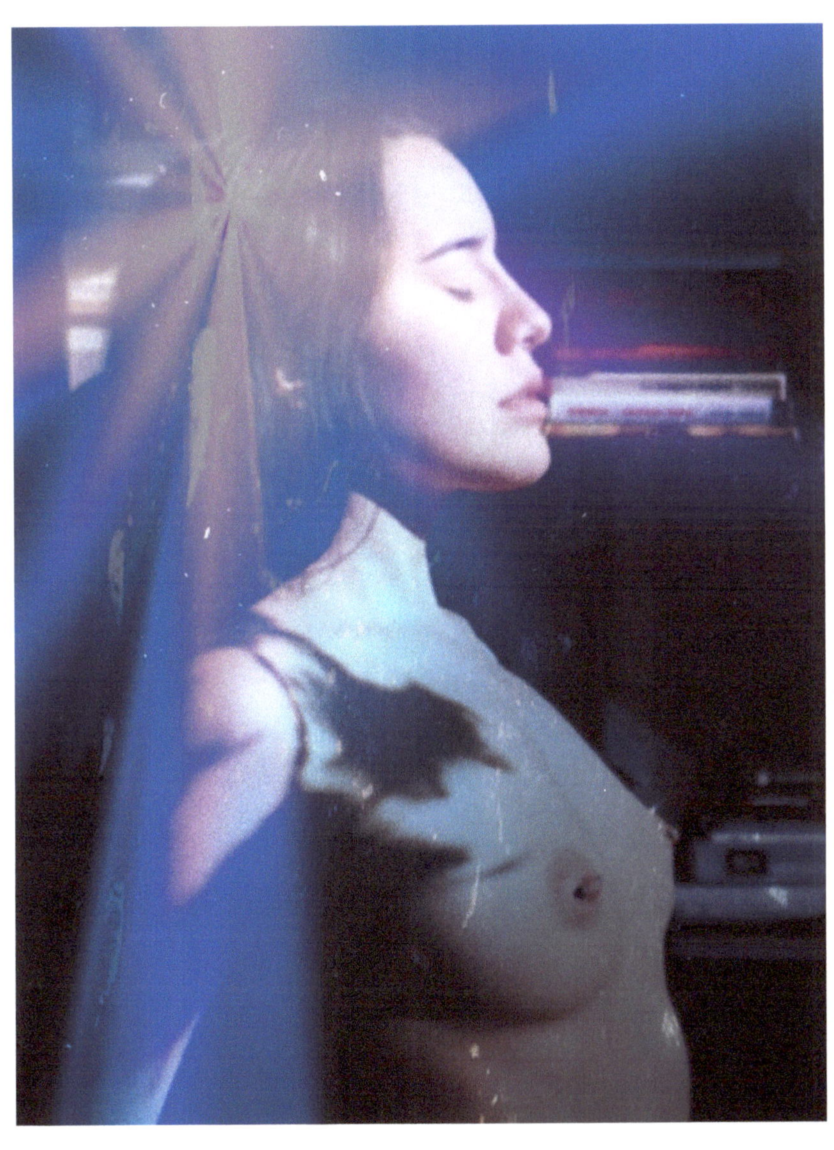

No dreamcatcher can contain her
the oceans within flow like stardust, coloring emptiness
oh, what I would do to be caught defenseless
in her celestial undertow

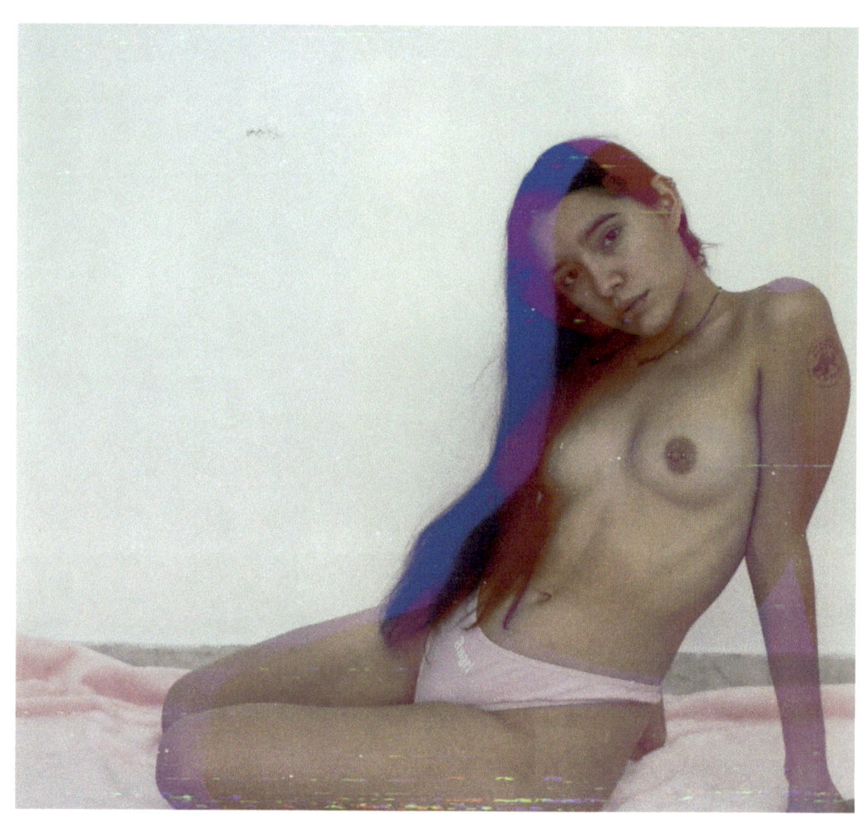

She is the painting
that film wishes it could capture

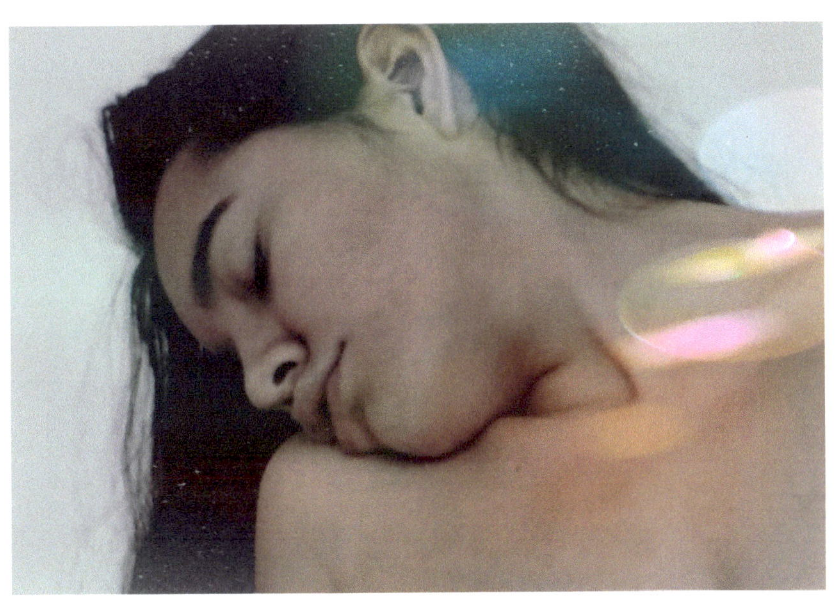

Gentle dreams
soft findings
on beaches unseen
'neath the eyelid
counting butterflies
instead of sheep
infinitesimal constellations
stippling midnight hair
a stroke, a caress
to perceive her
is to feel Love's lips

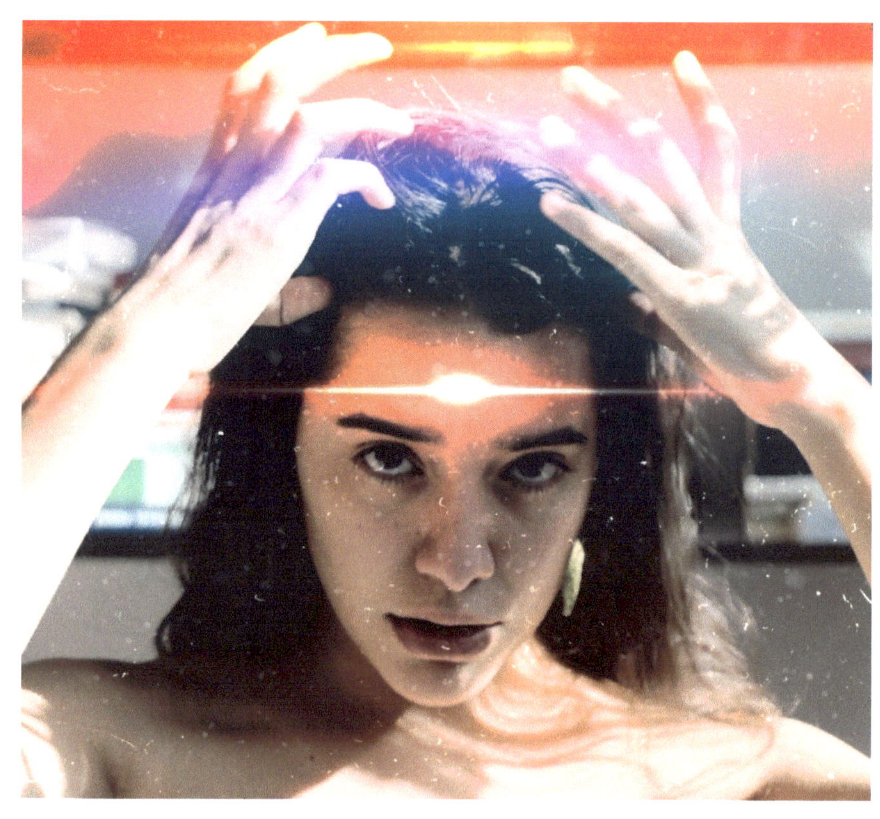

Make no mistake
you are a destroyer of worlds
wearer of stolen crowns
the bringer of light in depths of redness
there is no soul you cannot claim
no earth you cannot conquer
I see the frailty of clouds in you
but I also tremble in awe
at the storms they are capable
of unleashing upon us all
never underestimate your potential
even annihilation can be beautiful

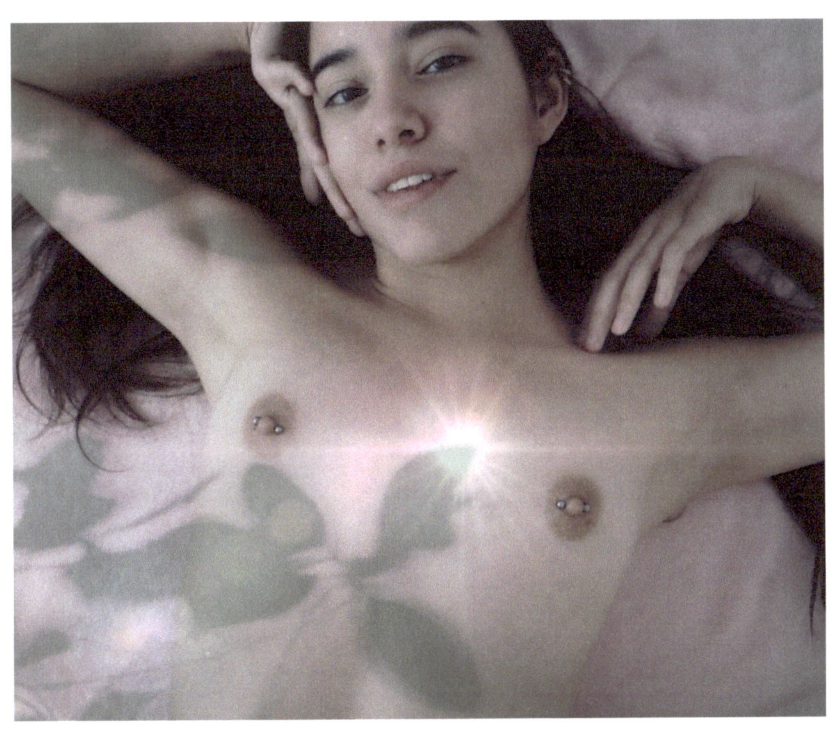

The leaves in your garden
glow fiercely
with a powerful gentleness
the same soft scintillation
that glimmers
through your smallest smile

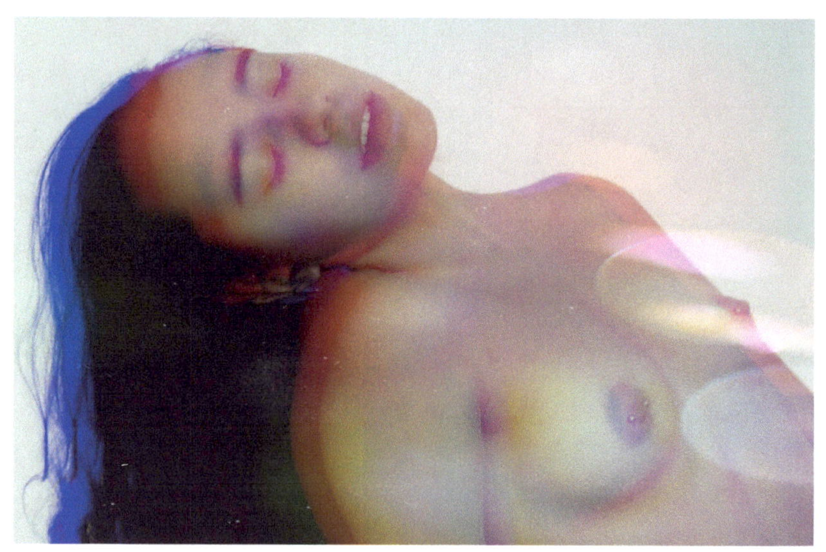

Acquiesce as the waves
surge over and through you
there is no denying
that you weren't meant for this realm
so let the malleable currents
carry you into the ether
back where you belong
a celestial empire
your rightful throne

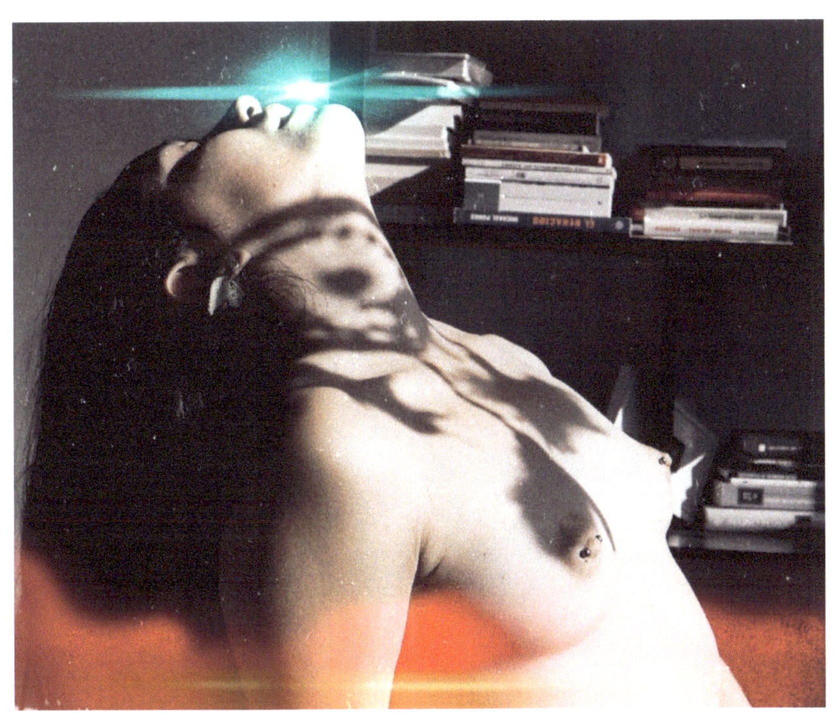

Change is here.
Don't just watch her breathe,
watch her come undone.
Watch her writhe,
like a curtain in the wind.
Feel the power
wash over you as you witness
her transcendence.
There is beauty,
and then there is this.

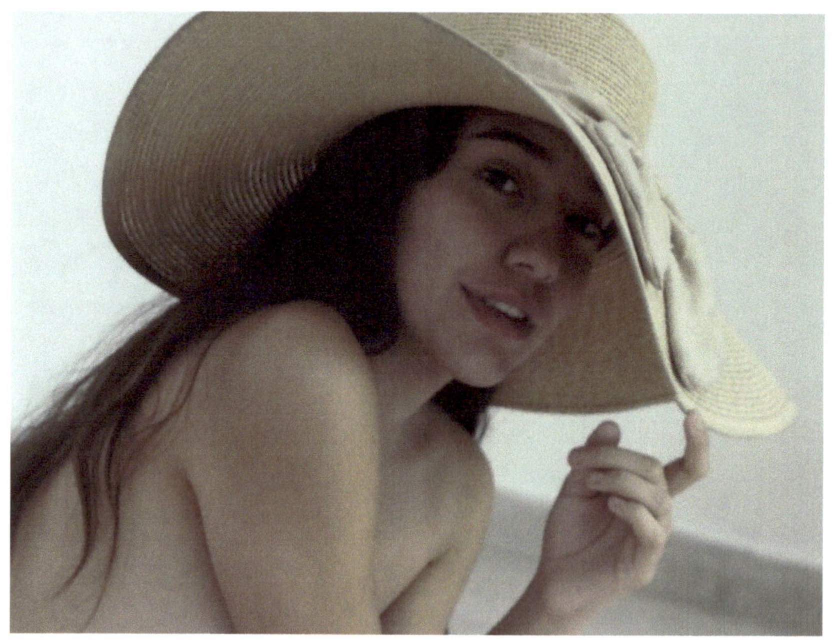

"What delights us in visible beauty is the invisible."

Marie von Ebner-Eschenbach

www.ingramcontent.com/pod-product-compliance
Lightning Source LLC
Chambersburg PA
CBHW040949110726
48006CB00007B/1325